Becoming Warriors

Work Book

Peta Taberner

Becoming Warriors Workbook © Peta Taberner

First published by Bekker Media for Hope Ministries International 2025
www.hopeministriesinternational.com.au

All rights reserved. Without limiting the rights under copyright reserved above, no part of this publication may be reproduced, stored in or introduced into a database and retrieval system or transmitted in any form or any means (electronic, mechanical, photocopying, recording or otherwise) without the prior written permission of both the owner of the copyright and the above publishers. The only exception is brief quotations in printed reviews.

First printed by IngramSpark in 2025
ISBN: 978-0-9756199-3-3

eISBN: 978-0-9756199-4-0

A copy of Becoming Warriors Workbook is lodged with the National Library Australia.

Unless otherwise specified, all scripture taken from the New King James Version®. Copyright © 1982 by Thomas Nelson. Used by permission. All rights reserved.

Scripture quotations marked NLT are taken from the Holy Bible, New Living Translation. Copyright © 1996, 2004, 2015 by Tyndale House Foundation. Used by permission of Tyndale House Ministries, Carol Stream, Illinois 60188. All rights reserved.

Scripture quotations marked TPT are taken from The Passion Translation®. Copyright © 2017, 2018 by Passion & Fire Ministries, Inc. Used by permission. All rights reserved. ThePassionTranslation.com.

Scripture quotations taken from the Amplified® Bible (AMP), Copyright © 2015 by The Lockman Foundation. Used by permission.

CONTENTS

Introduction 1

Chapter 1 Basic Soldier Training 3

Chapter 2 The Bible
(Our Training Manual) 25

Chapter 3 Putting Aside Distractions 33

Chapter 4 Allow The Pruning 41

Chapter 5 Armour Of God 49

Chapter 6 Fortify The Mind 57

Chapter 7 Oil In Our Lamps 63

Chapter 8 Fighting FROM Victory 71

Chapter 9 Naturally Supernatural 77

Chapter 10 Habits And Characteristics Of A Warrior Of God
(recap + extras) 83

INTRODUCTION

"THE CHURCH IS NOT AN AUDIENCE TO BE ENTERTAINED; IT IS AN ARMY TO BE EMPOWERED!" J.D. GREEAR

The Bible says in 1 Timothy 6:12, *"Fight the good fight of faith, lay hold on eternal life, to which you were also called and have confessed the good confession in the presence of many witnesses."*

When we become Christians, (when we give our lives to God and become "born again"), we are actually signing up to be part of an army - we are enlisting in the army of God! There are so many references in the Word that relate to the army of God, to us being soldiers, many of which I will quote and unpack throughout this workbook.

What army doesn't need training? I have never been in the army or participated in any training myself, but I have studied some of what they do, and I know the training is pretty intense!!

Those who join the army definitely do not turn up just once a week for training; they actually live on the army base and undergo extreme and rigorous training every day, disciplining their bodies, putting aside distractions, learning new skills and refining them, practicing with their weapons and undergoing pressure in different circumstances in preparation for war.

Why do we think it would be any different for a follower of Christ who has joined the army of God? Without the appropriate discipline, training and pressure, we will not be equipped when we face the enemy; we will be ineffective and easily defeated.

There is a war in the heavenlies. We have a real enemy who wants to steal, kill and destroy, who strategises to undermine and overthrow the saints, who is constantly making evil plans to attack the body of Christ.

My prayer is that, through the pages of this book, as you study the word and dig deeper in the Scriptures, you will hear the voice of the Lord and the warrior that you are called to be will rise up, become clothed in the full armour of God, take up the weapons you have been given and step into place in the Kingdom Army!

"Proclaim this among the nations: "Prepare for war! Wake up the mighty men, let all the men of war draw near, let them come up." (Joel 3:9)

"you can't fight without knowing what you're fighting for."

CHAPTER 1
BASIC SOLDIER TRAINING

When we look at the basic training for soldiers in the army, we see three important steps:

1. Fundamentals (foundations, core values, beliefs, integrity, honour)
2. Physical (fitness, skills, weapons, targets, training, teamwork)
3. Mental (self-discipline, challenges, guarding values & ethics)

When looking at the army of God, we need to add that we must be prepared SPIRITUALLY as well!

1. FUNDAMENTALS

Foundations

It is imperative to lay the foundations first - you cannot build without foundations, you can't fight without knowing what you're fighting for!

The Bible speaks of solid foundations quite clearly, *""Therefore whoever hears these sayings of Mine, and does them, I will liken him to a wise man who built his house on the rock: and the rain descended, the floods came, and the winds blew and beat on that house; and it did not fall, for it was founded on the rock. But everyone who hears these sayings of Mine, and does not do them, will be like a foolish man who built his house on the sand: and the rain descended, the floods came, and the winds blew and beat on that house; and it fell. And great was its fall.""*

Making sure we have a firm foundation - for example, knowing not only what we believe, but why we believe it, having clear values and morals, being a person of integrity and honour, will give us the stability to stand against the enemy. Without this foundation, we will crumble when the attacks come.

When you look at some of the basic foundations of the Christian faith you have:

- God/Trinity: we believe in the One, True and living God who consists of three persons, God the Father, God the Son and God the Holy Spirit.
- The Bible: we believe that the Bible is the inspired written word of God.
- Life, Death and Resurrection of Christ: we believe Jesus was born of a virgin, lived a sinless life, then died and rose again.
- Sin: we believe that we are born in sin because of the fall, and salvation comes only through Jesus Christ.

Search out the scriptures, ensure you have a solid foundation, knowing not only WHAT you believe but WHY you believe!

Core values/beliefs

Once our foundations are solid, we can then build our core values upon them - those beliefs we view as being of utmost importance. The principles that guide our actions. Our core values need to be founded on the Bible. For instance, they could emphasise love and forgiveness, compassion, humility and faithfulness. These core values will guide how we live our lives and how we interact with others; they will help us define our boundaries and prioritise what truly matters to us.

Churches often have core values they focus on, for example, Fire Church Ministries has these core values:

- Love and Presence

- The Word

- Empowerment

Integrity

The dictionary meaning of integrity is the quality of being honest and having strong moral principles. I believe for a Christian or follower of Jesus, integrity means much more. Integrity is the consistent and uncompromising adherence to doing what is right in the eyes of God. It's a moral compass that guides us down the narrow path leading to eternal life. It is doing right, even when no-one is watching. It is staying honest, accountable and transparent.

Walking in integrity means staying true to the principles of faith; it involves reflecting the word of God and the teachings of Jesus in both our public life and our private lives.

Proverbs 10:9 says, *"He who walks in integrity and with moral character walks securely, But he who takes a crooked way will be discovered and punished."*

And in Psalm 25:21, *"May integrity and honesty protect me, for I put my hope in you."*

Honour

The Bible speaks a lot about honour. Honouring God, honouring leadership, honouring our parents, honouring our fellow brothers and sisters in the Lord, honouring elders, honouring authority.

Honour is so important. Honouring God and respecting His sovereignty over ALL is the foundation of Biblical honour, *"Who is like the Lord our God, who is seated on high, who looks far down on the heavens and the earth?"* (Psalm 113:5).

Honouring others stems from the belief that all people are created in God's image, *"So God created human beings in his own image. In the image of God he created them; male and female he created them."* (Genesis 1:27 NLT)

Romans 12:10 says to, *"Be devoted to one another in brotherly love. Outdo yourselves in honouring one another."*

Honouring our fathers and mothers is explicitly tied to living long and having things go well with us (Exodus 20:12).

Honouring leadership and authority is essential for growth. Hebrews 13:17 says to *"Obey your [spiritual] leaders and submit to them [recognising their authority over you], for they are keeping watch over your souls and continually guarding your spiritual welfare as those who will give an account [of their stewardship of you]. Let them do this with joy and not with grief and groans, for this would be of no benefit to you"* (AMP).

In 1 Thessalonians 5:12, we're told to *"honour those who are your leaders in the Lord's work. They work hard among you and give you spiritual guidance"* (NLT).

God is the one who puts leadership in place to help us mature and grow, to call out the gold in us, to push us towards our calling and to lead us out of our comfort zones, to help us become good leaders ourselves.

We need to submit ourselves to their leading, trusting that they are hearing from God, seeking His will and following His direction.

Sometimes leaders make choices that we don't agree with; sometimes leaders get it wrong, but you can have honouring, honest conversations with your leaders when this happens. Having a face-to-face conversation with a leader is more honouring than criticising or gossiping about them behind their backs.

When it comes to walking in honour, **Jesus is our model.** Jesus is the ultimate example of obedience, servanthood and humility. In His life on earth, He was constantly submitted to His Father, desiring only to please Him and bring Him glory. Have a look below at just some of the statements Jesus made.

"I do nothing of Myself; but as My Father taught Me, I speak these things" (John 8:28).

"I always do those things that please Him" (John 8:29).

"For I have come down from heaven, not to do My own will, but the will of Him who sent me" (John 6:38).

"For I have not spoken on My own authority; but the Father who sent Me gave Me a command, what I should say and what I should speak" (John 12:49).

QUESTIONS

1. What are your foundational beliefs?

2. What are your core values?

3. In what ways can I grow/improve in integrity?

QUESTIONS

4. In what ways can I grow/improve in honour?

2. PHYSICAL

Health

In the natural it is obviously better to be physically fit and healthy. Training as a soldier includes a lot of physical exercise as well as training with weapons, learning new skills and working in teams.

In 1 Corinthians chapter 6, the Bible tells us that our *"bodies are temples of the Holy Spirit...not our own but bought with a price."*

Since our bodies are His temple, it's important to honour God by making choices that promote physical health and fitness as a form of worship and gratitude to the Lord.

Having times of rest are essential for longevity. In Genesis, after God created the world, He rested. Rest is definitely something we need - having a Sabbath day each week, carving out time for holidays, creating a healthy balance between work and rest, recognising that both are necessary to flourish.

Eating healthy foods and having a balanced diet, exercising and resting, avoiding harmful substances; the Bible speaks of all this and emphasises caring for our bodies.

Skill

We are each gifted (by God) with different skills and abilities, each called into different areas, each given different positions in this Kingdom army, with different roles or parts to play.

In order to operate fully in these skills, we need to train and/or practice them. To become good at playing a musical instrument takes time, lessons, and plenty of practice to strengthen and improve our skill. The same applies to singing, or cooking, or preaching, or any other gift, skill or ability.

We are the body of Christ. Just as a baby grows and learns to walk and talk and use different parts of its body, so too do we need to grow and learn how to function in our particular gift as part of the body of Christ.

Weapons

In Ephesians 6 Paul talks about the armour of God, (which we will look at further in chapter 5), and mentions the sword of the Spirit - which is the word of God (the Bible). The Word is our weapon. Jesus defeated the enemy in the desert by the word of God - *"It is written..."*

The Bible is just one of our weapons. We are also given other weapons, one of which is found at the end of those verses in Ephesians - and that is prayer! The Bible says that, *"the effective, fervent prayer of a righteous man availeth much."* (James 5:16), and *"Pray without ceasing"* (1Thessalonians 5:17).

We need to use prayer as a weapon, not a wish list! Let's not pray just to request things from God, but let's use our prayers to speak into situations and circumstances.

Life and death are in the power of our tongue (Proverbs 18:21). Our tongue is a powerful weapon!

We can use our words to wound or to heal, to speak truth or to lie, to inflict harm or for protection. God Himself used words to speak the world into existence!

Another weapon we have is our testimony. It says in Revelation 12:11 (AMP), *"And they overcame and conquered him because of the blood of the Lamb and because of the word of their testimony, for they did not love their life and renounce their faith even when faced with death."*

Prophecy is also a weapon. 1 Timothy 1 :17 says, *"This charge I commit to you, son Timothy, according to the prophecies previously made concerning you, that by them you may wage the good warfare,"*

When we read prophecy in the Word or when we receive prophetic words, we can use them as a weapon against the enemy. Prophecies are given as directives to take action and fulfill God's purposes. When spoken or declared, these prophetic words can be used to combat negative circumstances, reinforce faith, and align us with God's will over our lives. Speaking prophetic words aloud reinforces faith and helps us to overcome doubt or fear.

Prophetic words provide a sense of purpose and direction and help to anchor us to God's plans and purposes, even during difficult times.

The Name of Jesus is a powerful weapon - the Bible says, *"at the name of Jesus EVERY KNEE SHALL BOW"* (Phillipians 2:10, emphasis added), and not just on earth, but it says, *"those in heaven, on earth and under the earth!"*

Jesus is the Name above every other name. Luke 10:17 says, *"The seventy returned with joy, saying, "Lord, even the demons are subject to us in Your name.""*

We cannot win against the enemy in our own strength, but Jesus has given us His Name, *"And these signs will follow those who believe: IN MY NAME they will cast out demons..."* (Mark 16:17, emphasis added)

I mentioned the verse in Revelations that speaks of *"the blood of the Lamb"* as a weapon along with our testimony. The blood of Jesus is both an offensive (legal basis for overcoming the enemy), and defensive (shield against attacks), weapon.

The blood of Jesus cleanses us (1 John 1:7), justifies us (Romans 5:9), sanctifies us (Hebrews 13:12), redeems us (Ephesians 1:7).

QUESTIONS

5. Am I physically fit and healthy?

6. In what ways can I improve my physical health?

7. What are some skills/gifts that God has given me?

QUESTIONS

8. In what ways can I grow in these skills/gifts?

9. Do I know how to use the weapons God has given me?

10. What weapons can I use/develop more?

Targets

We must know the target! Those who are serving alongside us are NOT our enemy!

Not only do soldiers try and prepare *themselves* for war, but they also study their target (the enemy). Learning the different tactics and strategies that the enemy uses will help prepare us for any attacks.

We can see in the Bible that the enemy continually tries to sow seeds of doubt or challenges the truth of the Bible. Learning to fortify our mind by knowing what is written in the Word will help to defeat the enemy in this area.

When Jesus was tempted, He defeated the enemy with the truth of the Word - *"It is written…"*

Knowing the target involves not only knowing their location and capabilities (the weapons and methods they use) but also understanding the motivations and intentions of the enemy. Finding the weak points or areas they are susceptible to attack.

The Bible says that the enemy (Satan - the devil), *"comes to steal, kill and destroy"*, so we know the intention, but we also know that Jesus *"came to give life, and life more abundantly!"* (John 10:10). Knowing also that we are *"seated with Him in Heavenly places, far above principalities and powers of this world"* and we are *"more than conquerors"* through Jesus because He has already won the victory!

Training

1 Corinthians 9:27 says, *"But I discipline my body and bring it into subjection, lest, when I have preached to others, I myself should become disqualified."*

Spiritual disciplines such as reading and studying the Bible, prayer, fasting, serving, submission, worship, fellowship, all cultivate growth in faith and relationship with God and are essential for us to mature in Christ.

As well as spiritual training, physical and mental training is also important, as mentioned earlier.

Without consistent training our bodies become unfit; so too in the spirit. Without spiritual disciplines, our lives become lethargic and complacent. It is our job to keep the fire burning.

2 Timothy 1:6 says, *"Therefore I remind you to stir up the gift of God which is in you through the laying on of my hands."*

Teamwork

As mentioned above, our fellow soldiers are not our enemy. Don't shoot your brother or sister in the trenches. We need to work together as a team, linking arms like shields touching to form an impenetrable barrier!

Support and encourage one another, pray together, study the Word together, honour others above yourselves. Romans 12:10 says to *"outdo one another in showing honour"*.

The Bible says we are one body with every part having a vital role to play. We don't need to compete with those who are on the same team, instead we complement (complete or bring out the best) in one another, each of us contributing uniquely in the role we have to play.

We all see in part.

Imagine if there were a five people seated around a table with a bottle of Coca Cola in the centre with a label, as below. Each person would notice a different part of the label on that bottle. One could say that the label says "Coca-Cola", another would say it says, "share a Coke with Ryan", still another would say, "I can see the Nutrition facts and ingredients" or "I can only see a barcode". Each of them would be correct, but they are only seeing part of the label.

But, if they work together as a team, they could piece together the whole label!

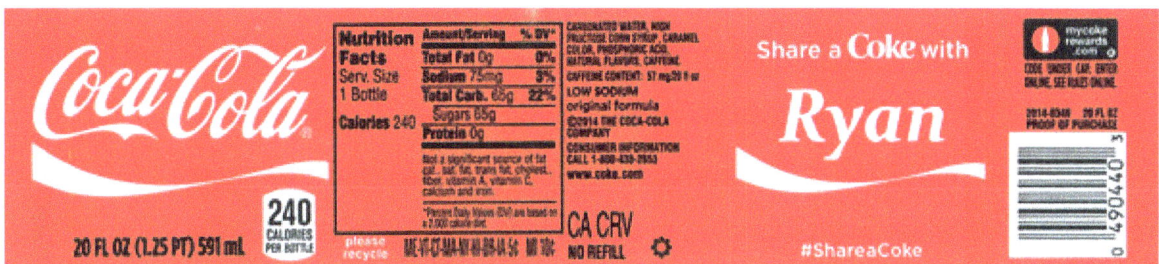

No matter what part we are in the Body of Christ, or what position we are in, we are given grace for that role, and when we work together with our eyes fixed on Jesus, empowered by the Holy Spirit, we are an effective army against the enemy.

Make it normal to call out each other's graces and encourage one another in the different gifts and abilities. A culture of competition will die amidst a culture of encouragement.

"For we are God's fellow workers; you are God's field, you are God's building. According to the grace of God, which was given to me, as a wise master builder I have laid the foundation, and another builds on it. But let each one take heed how he builds on it." (1 Corinthians 3:9-10)

"But to each one of us grace was given according to the measure of Christ's gift." (Ephesians 4:7)

"from whom the whole body, joined and knit together by what every joint supplies, according to the effective working by which every part does its share, causes growth of the body for the edifying of itself in love." (Ephesiains 4:16)

QUESTIONS

11. Do I know my targets, tactics, strategies and capabilities?

12. What sort of disciplines do I practise to train for the battle?

13. Where do you think God is training and upskilling you in this season?

QUESTIONS

14. Am I a good team-player?

15. When was the last time you encouraged the other recruits in Gods Army?

3. MENTAL

As well as physical training, training our minds is so important. Later in this study we will go into more depth about "fortifying the mind", but just as with physical training, mental training also starts with self-discipline. Bringing our thoughts in line with the word of God.

About guarding our minds, Phillipians 4:7 says, *"And the peace of God [that peace which reassures the heart, that peace] which transcends all understanding, [that peace which] stands **guard** over your hearts and your **minds** in Christ Jesus [is yours]."*

Not every thought that enters our mind is our own thought. Learning to take every thought captive takes discipline; retraining our thinking takes practice.

The enemy will often bring thoughts to your mind - thoughts of temptation, critical thoughts of yourself, thoughts of sin, negative thoughts, etc. and he will pose them in such a way that you believe they are your thoughts or desires.

Here is a Biblical example of this happening; *"It was during supper, when the devil had already put [the thought of] betraying Jesus into the heart of Judas Iscariot, Simon's son,"* (John 13:2)

There are many keys that we can use to guard or fortify our mind that we will look at in Chapter 6.

SPIRITUAL

In the army of God, there is one more essential preparation we need and that is to be **spiritually** prepared. We can be physically and mentally ready, but without the power of the Holy Spirit, we are fighting in our own strength! We must have the Holy Spirit to defeat the enemy's plans.

In Acts, before Jesus ascended to heaven, He told His followers to wait for the Holy Spirit. If Jesus told His followers to wait for the promise of the Holy Spirit, what makes us think we can do this without the Holy Spirit?

Too often we try to serve God without God. What do I mean by this?

There is a difference between the Person of the Holy Spirit and the POWER of the Holy Spirit.

If we try to walk this journey without the power, we will soon burn out!

Galatians 3:3 says, *"Are you so foolish and senseless? Having begun [your new life by faith] with the Spirit, are you now being perfected and reaching spiritual maturity by the flesh [that is, by your own works and efforts to keep the Law]?"*

When we become baptised in the Holy Spirit, as the Bible says (Matthew 3:11, Luke 3:16), just like they were at Pentecost, we become filled with the Holy Spirit! But if you look through the book of Acts, this was not a one-time event; there are numerous places where it says they were filled AGAIN with the Holy Spirit.

We must be continually filled. The Holy Spirit is the power of God,

He is our comforter (Acts 9:31),

He is our teacher (John 14:26),

He is our guide (John 16:13),

He is our strength (Ephesians 3:6),

He is our help (Romans 8:26).

He convicts (John 16:1),

He reveals (1 Corinthians 2:10),

He instructs (Acts 8:29),

He renews us (Titus 3:5),

He gives us access to the Father (Ephesians 2:18).

He brings joy (1 Thessalonians 1:6),

He is our peace (Ephesians 2:14),

He sanctifies us (2 Thessalonians 2:13),

He empowers us (Acts 1:8).

He transforms us (2 Corinthians 3:18),

He brings freedom (Romans 8:2),

He seals us (Ephesians 1:13),

He prays for us (Romans 8:26)!

QUESTIONS

16. Am I mentally prepared for battle?

17. What can I do to improve my thought-life?

QUESTIONS

18. Am I spiritually prepared for battle?

19. In what ways can I invite the Holy Spirit in more?

REFLECTIONS

REFLECTIONS

"...our source of wisdom, instruction and disciplines."

CHAPTER 2
THE BIBLE (OUR TRAINING MANUAL)

Psalm 144:1 says, *"Blessed be the Lord my Rock, Who trains my hands for war, And my fingers for battle.*

Verse 2- *"My lovingkindness and my fortress, My high tower and my deliverer, My shield and the One in whom I take refuge, Who subdues my people under me."*

God Himself is the One who trains us for war, but He is also our protector and our defence (our fortress, our high tower, our deliverer, our shield).

The Bible says that God trains us for war. How? We are given a training manual, the BIBLE.

*"Study and do your best to present yourself to God approved, a workman [tested by trial] who has no reason to be ashamed, accurately handling and skilfully teaching the word of truth. All Scripture is God-breathed [given by divine inspiration] and is profitable for instruction, for conviction [of sin], for correction [of error and restoration to obedience], for **training** in righteousness [learning to live in conformity to God's will, both publicly and privately—behaving honourably with personal integrity and moral courage]; so that the man of God may be complete and proficient, **outfitted and thoroughly equipped** for every good work."* (2 Timothy 3:15-17, emphasis mine).

The word of God contains all the instruction we need for EVERY situation, circumstance and enemy attack we face. The Bible is our guide for EVERY area of our lives - parenting, marriage, money, sin, family, our speech, our actions, humility, our health, morals, pride, self-control, and even sex!

The Bible gives us guidelines that are applicable regardless of time, place or person. It provides guidance on how to live our lives in a way that aligns with God's will. It is a source of instruction, wisdom, and disciplines that help shape us to be more effective as disciples and ministers.

James 1:21-25 says, *"Therefore lay aside all filthiness and overflow of wickedness, and receive with meekness the implanted word, which is able to save your souls. But be doers of the word, and not hearers only, deceiving yourselves. For if anyone is a hearer of the word and not a doer, he is like a man observing his natural face in a mirror; for he observes himself, goes away, and immediately forgets what kind of man he was. But he who looks into the perfect law of liberty and continues in it and is not a forgetful hearer but a doer of the work, this one will be blessed in what he does."*

A manual can save so much time, effort and energy, but in order for it to be beneficial it must be read and the instructions followed.

The Bible provides principles and examples for living a life pleasing to God. It equips us and provides a foundation for our spiritual growth, however, in order to be shaped by the Word, we need to apply the Scripture to our lives. It is not enough to simply read the Bible; we must act on it. Applying the biblical principles contained in the pages of the word of God will bring about the promises of God contained in those very same pages.

Putting into practice what we read in the word of God will take effort, self-discipline, persistence and endurance. Doing a regular Bible study or devotion can be a great start. Journaling and meditating on specific verses or books of the Bible or people of the Bible, having a reading plan with reflection and applications - all of these will help with applying the scriptures to our lives.

Setting aside time daily, without interruption, is important to study the Word. Be consistent, even if you start off with a short amount of time each day. Be patient and don't get discouraged, continue to seek God's guidance and wisdom. Pray and ask the Holy Spirit to help you, listen to what He is saying or highlighting to you, then focus on the application. Ultimately, the goal is to allow God's Spirit to transform us as we read and understand the Bible.

"For the word of God is living and active and full of power [making it operative, energizing, and effective]. It is sharper than any two-edged sword, penetrating as far as the division of the soul and spirit [the completeness of a person], and of both joints and marrow [the deepest parts of our nature], exposing and judging the very thoughts and intentions of the heart." (Hebrews 4:12, AMP)

The word of God is a powerful weapon when we read it, meditate on it, obey and put it into practice. The Bible says it is sharper than any two-edged sword; but we must know what it says for it to be effective in defeating the enemy. When we know what it says and speak it out with conviction - only then will it cut down the enemy's lies, break through the enemy's attacks, and push back the enemy's advances.

QUESTIONS

1. How often do I read/meditate on/study the Bible?

2. Can I improve on this? In what ways?

QUESTIONS

3. When I read the Word am I obeying it and applying it to my life?

4. Do I use the Word of God as a weapon against the enemy's lies?

QUESTIONS

5. Do any Bible verses come to mind that you can use as a weapon in this particular season of your life?

REFLECTIONS

REFLECTIONS

REFLECTIONS

REFLECTIONS

"...look away from every-thing else..."

CHAPTER 3
PUTTING ASIDE DISTRACTIONS

One thing that is crucial in putting aside distractions - we must keep our gaze fixed on our Lord and Saviour, Jesus Christ.

Hebrews 12:2 says, *"Therefore, since we are surrounded by so great a cloud of witnesses [who by faith have testified to the truth of God's absolute faithfulness], stripping off every unnecessary weight and the sin which so easily and cleverly entangles us, let us run with endurance and active persistence the race that is set before us, [looking away from all that will distract us and] focusing our eyes on Jesus, who is the Author and Perfecter of faith [the first incentive for our belief and the One who brings our faith to maturity], who for the joy [of accomplishing the goal] set before Him endured the cross, disregarding the shame, and sat down at the right hand of the throne of God [revealing His deity, His authority, and the completion of His work]."*

How do we fix our gaze on Jesus?

By stripping off every weight - every weight of sin, every weight of disobedience, every weight of distraction, every weight of bondage (separating ourselves from these things)

By enduring with active persistence, (it takes effort);

- enduring meaning: long lasting, continuing, unceasing, abiding.

- persistence meaning: steady determination, tenacious, perseverance, continuous.

By looking away from everything else - removing things from our gaze; things we watch on TV, things we read, looking away from the world (turning away).

By looking at Him - over and over and over again. Look at Him in His word, look at Him in prayer, look at Him in worship, look at Him in others, look at Him in creation ("Looking" in original Greek means to properly stare, to experience, to discern clearly, to see with the mind and with the eyes, to perceive, to behold).

In 2 Timothy 2:4 in the Passion translation, *"For every soldier called to active duty must divorce himself from the distractions of this world so that he may fully satisfy the one who chose him."*

It's all too easy to become distracted by so many things! Distracted by sin, distracted by wealth or opportunities, distracted by our own feelings or by the opinions of others, distracted by technology, distracted by circumstances, even distracted by serving or ministry!

The enemy works hard to get people to take their eyes off the mission.

I love the book of Song of Solomon where it speaks about Dove's eyes.

"Behold, how beautiful you are, my darling, Behold, how beautiful you are! Your eyes are dove's eyes." (Song of Solomon 1:15, AMP)

Most birds have peripheral vision (meaning you can see things outside your direct line of sight), but the interesting thing about the dove is that it has singular vision. In other words, it is only able to focus on one thing at a time. When a dove fixes its gaze upon its mate, it is not distracted by any activities around it.

Here in the beautiful love song of Solomon, the lover, speaking to the beloved, he speaks of her eyes as being "dove's eyes". In other words, Solomon says about his beloved, "she only has eyes for me!"

I wonder if our King, Jesus could say that we, His bride, has dove's eyes? I wonder if in our own lives we only have eyes for Jesus! To have dove's eyes means to be captured and captivated by Him alone.

Or are we…DISTRACTED?

In Matthew 14, Jesus had just fed the 5000, the disciples were out in the boat, there was a bit of a storm happening and Jesus comes walking towards them and they're afraid (they thought it was a ghost).

Peter yells out, *"Lord if it's you tell me to come."* Jesus says, *"Come."*

Peter, fixes His eyes on Jesus, jumps out and starts walking on the water.

All is fine until Peter takes his eyes off Jesus and becomes distracted by the wind and waves, and he begins to sink. Verse 30 says, *"But when he saw [the effects of] the wind, he was frightened, and he began to sink, and he cried out, "Lord, save me!""*

If we are not vigilant and allow the influx of little distractions into our lives, we may unknowingly start to sink in our spiritual walk with Christ and lose sight of the finishing line.

Psalm 68:8 says, *"I have set the Lord always before me…because He is at my right hand I will not be moved."*

In his wonderful vision in Isaiah chapter 6, the prophet sees many things: a throne, cherubim, a robe, an altar, a coal, the smoke of God's presence. All these things are wonderful. But notice how he begins his description, *"In the year that King Uzziah died, I saw the Lord"*. To Isaiah, everything else was eclipsed by the fact that he saw the Lord!

Once you have seen the Lord nothing else can compare and nothing else will claim your attention except Him.

QUESTIONS

1. Do I allow myself to be distracted?

2. Can I improve on this? In what ways?

QUESTIONS

3. Do I set aside time daily to spend with the Lord without ANY distractions?

4. Can I improve on this? In what ways?

REFLECTIONS

REFLECTIONS

REFLECTIONS

"for the Lord disciplines and corrects those whom he loves."

CHAPTER 4
ALLOW THE PRUNING

Allow yourself to grow; do not bypass the tests and trials.

James 1:2-4 says, (AMP)

"Consider it nothing but joy, my brothers and sisters, whenever you fall into various trials. Be assured that the testing of your faith [through experience] produces endurance [leading to spiritual maturity, and inner peace]. And let endurance have its perfect result and do a thorough work, so that you may be perfect and completely developed [in your faith], lacking in nothing."

And this scripture, Romans 5:3-4 (AMP)

"And not only this, but [with joy] let us exult in our sufferings and rejoice in our hardships, knowing that hardship (distress, pressure, trouble) produces patient endurance; and endurance, proven character (spiritual maturity); and proven character, hope and confident assurance [of eternal salvation]."

We all experience pressure, trials, tests, hard times, but we need to use these times to be trained, to grow, so that we can be the warriors that the Lord is calling us to be!

Let's use these times to allow the Lord to show us the areas in our lives we need to deal with, the things we need to overcome. If we don't keep pressing in and growing, building our character, then we will become stagnant and eventually lukewarm.

If we feed and water a plant, it will grow, but plants also need to be pruned, and the dead bits taken off in order to maintain strong healthy growth. The Bible talks about us in this regard, John 15:2, *"Every branch in Me that does not bear fruit, He takes away; and every branch that continues to bear fruit, He [repeatedly] prunes, so that it will bear more fruit [even richer and finer fruit]."*

Your character and resilience are forged out of the trials you face; from the testing of your faith, trust is born. Once you come to completely trust in the One who holds your very life in His Hands, you are confident that His ways are perfect and that He is truly faithful.

It is only when you need Jesus to step in as your Saviour, that you truly understand what it means to be saved. Sometimes the enemy may think he is drowning you with problems, but really, he is presenting the perfect opportunity for God to prove His faithfulness.

In Hebrews 12:6 (AMP) it says, *"For the Lord disciplines and corrects those whom He loves, And He punishes every son whom He receives and welcomes [to His heart]."*

The Lord wants us to grow and mature into all He has called us to be, however, just as we correct and discipline our children so too the Father needs to correct and discipline us. This doesn't always feel great; what discipline does? But on the other side of the correction is righteousness, grace, peace, blessings and abundance.

Lean closer to the Lord throughout the tests and trials, throughout the discipline, throughout the character building, knowing that He is a good Father!

"Many are the afflictions of the righteous, But the Lord delivers him out of them all." (Psalm 34:19)

The Bible doesn't say that no weapon will be formed against you...it says that those weapons will not prosper! (Isaiah 54:17)

We will most definitely face storms in life. Here are three examples from the Bible about storms that were faced - I would encourage you to read through them and see how they can be applied to your life in the situations you are facing.

1. We've all heard the story of Jonah and the whale!

Jonah's storm, which can be found in the book of Jonah, was a result of his disobedience. The Lord had given Jonah an assignment which he was unwilling to carry out.

"Now the word of the Lord came to Jonah the son of Amittai, saying, "Arise, go to Nineveh, that great city, and cry out against it; for their wickedness has come up before Me." But Jonah arose to flee to Tarshish from the presence of the Lord. He went down to Joppa, and found a ship going to Tarshish; so he paid the fare, and went down into it, to go with them to Tarshish from the presence of the Lord." (Jonah 1:1-3)

Once Jonah was on board the ship, a storm arose. Jonah, realising the storm was because of his disobedience, told the others on the boat to throw him overboard - which they did, and Jonah was swallowed by a big fish!

After three days and nights inside the belly of this fish, Jonah THEN cried out to God in repentance and the fish spat him out on dry land.

Jonah's repentance resulted in God giving him a second chance to go to Nineveh and warn the people of God's coming judgement.

2. The storm in Mark 4:35-41. Jesus had been with His disciples all day, teaching the multitudes and when the evening came, they all got in a boat to go to the other side of the sea, away from the crowds. Jesus went down for a sleep and a storm arose - there was no disobedience mentioned here, everyone was in the will of God. As the storm raged the boat began filling with water, yet Jesus kept on sleeping, undeterred. The disciples, however, went and woke Him up saying, *"Teacher, do you not care that we are perishing?" Then Jesus arose and rebuked the wind, and said to the sea, "Peace, be still!" And the wind ceased and there was a great calm. But He said to them, "Why are you so fearful? How is it that you have no faith?"* (Mark 4:38-40)

Jesus spoke to the storm, then addressed the fear of his disciples. Oftentimes, when we are in the will of God storms will come - sent to test our faith, to disrupt our peace or to bring fear. It's important that we know the Word and the promises of God, that we remain in peace knowing that God is faithful, and that we speak to the storm using the authority Jesus has given us!

3. Paul's storm in Acts 27 was the result of disobedience of others. Paul was in a ship heading to Rome and He had advised those in charge, saying, *"Men, I perceive that this voyage will end with disaster and much loss, not only of the cargo and ship, but also our lives." Nevertheless, the centurion was more persuaded by the helmsman and the owner of the ship than by the things spoken by Paul."* (Acts 27:10-11). The trip continued with a fierce storm for many days, cargo and tackle being thrown overboard and Paul's continued warnings.

Throughout this trip Paul urged them to listen and spoke what the Lord had told him. Paul prayed for them and stood in the gap for them until they listened to his advice. God answered his prayer and granted his request.

This storm reminds us of persevering in faith. Not everyone will take our advice, not everyone will listen to the Lord, not all our prayers will be answered right away and sometimes we will find ourselves in storms through no fault of our own but because of the actions of others. But rest assured, God hears us and will answer when we persevere and stand in faith.

All of these people had an assignment or calling to walk in. All faced storms to distract or stop their assignment; some as a result of their own actions or disobedience, others were attacks from the enemy and still others because of the actions of others.

There are many examples of storms, trials and tests throughout the Bible to encourage us. Storms will come, BUT God is in control.

QUESTIONS

1. Do I allow the pruning and discipline of the Lord or do I avoid it?

2. What tests/trials am I going through in this season?

QUESTIONS

3. How is the Lord developing my character through these trials?

4. In what ways have I allowed the Lord to prune me in the last six months?

5. What do we need to do in the storms we are facing today? Repent like Jonah? Speak the word like Jesus? Or persevere like Paul?

REFLECTIONS

REFLECTIONS

"we are in a battle. not against flesh and blood"

CHAPTER 5
ARMOUR OF GOD

God gives us all we need to enter the battle.

Ephesians 6:10-18, Armour of God:

"Finally, my brethren, be strong in the Lord and in the power of His might. Put on the whole armor of God, that you may be able to stand against the wiles of the devil. For we do not wrestle against flesh and blood, but against principalities, against powers, against the rulers of the darkness of this age, against spiritual hosts of wickedness in the heavenly places. Therefore, take up the whole armor of God, that you may be able to withstand in the evil day, and having done all, to stand. Stand therefore, having girded your waist with truth, having put on the breastplate of righteousness, and having shod your feet with the preparation of the gospel of peace; above all, taking the shield of faith with which you will be able to quench all the fiery darts of the wicked one. And take the helmet of salvation, and the sword of the Spirit, which is the word of God; praying always with all prayer and supplication in the Spirit, being watchful to this end with all perseverance and supplication for all the saints—"

We are in a battle. Not against flesh and blood - not against each other, not against those we disagree with, not against those who don't follow Christ, not against other religions, but against the devil! And we have been given the whole armour of God for this battle:

Belt of truth: the first piece of the armour. The belt of a Roman soldier was the foundation of his armour, holding together his breastplate and his sword. It was a symbol of power and status (the mark of a soldier), which the Roman soldier wore even while off duty.

Jesus said in John 14:6, *"I am the way, the TRUTH, and the life"*. Satan is the father of lies, he tries to manipulate and distort the truth, but he cannot stand against THE TRUTH. Without the truth, we are powerless, and the rest of the armour would be useless. We need to understand the truth of who God is, His character and His faithfulness.

Breastplate of righteousnes: the breastplate of a Roman soldier consisted of steel or iron that was curved to conform to the shape of the soldier's body and protected their upper torso, front and back as well as the tops of their shoulders. 2 Corinthians 5:21 (NKJV) says, *"For He made Him who knew no sin to be sin for us, that we might become the righteousness of God in Him."*

Shoes of the Gospel of peace: the assurance of the Gospel brings peace. A soldier's battle shoes were studded with nails or spikes so that he could hold his ground with his feet firmly planted, keeping his balance. In the same way we need the assurance (the peace) and confidence of our position, standing firm on the Word.

Shield of faith: the Roman shield of the time was called a *scutum* and it was as large as a door! It was used not just as protection but also to push back the enemy. These shields were often made of wood, and when wet could extinguish flaming arrows. In Ephesians 6:16 we are instructed to, *"above all, taking the shield of faith with which you will be able to quench all the fiery darts of the wicked one."* The shields could also be joined together to protect a group.

Helmet of salvation: protects our mind. Oftentimes the enemy will start with thoughts, and our mind can become a battlefield. We need to renew and fortify our minds.

Sword of the Spirit: all other armour is for our protection, but the sword of the Spirit (the word of God) is one of our weapons of attack. When we speak out the Word, it's like firing a missile!

A victorious soldier has not only studied his enemy's strategy - knowing where the enemy will attack, the direction the enemy is coming from, what weapons the enemy is using, but has also studied his own weaponry and defence. He knows what protection he has, he knows how to use his weapons, and he knows that his allies have his back and are there to fight alongside him. Everything we need has already been given to us; we just need to use it. After the different pieces of armour are listed, this passage of scripture goes on to talk about, "praying always" and "being watchful". You may have heard it said that "prayer is the engine room" or "without prayer nothing happens"; these sayings are so true.

We must be in constant communication with God. Prayer is not a monologue or a one-sided conversation; it is about a reciprocal relationship where we not only speak to God but also listen. It is not just to present our requests but to also hear God's voice, listen for His feedback and guidance. Prayer is not something we do once a day or once a week; it's an on-going conversation with our Father.

QUESTIONS

1. Do I understand how to use the armour of God?

2. What piece (or pieces) of the armour do I forget to use?

QUESTIONS

3. How can I improve in using the armour of God?

4. How often do I pray?

QUESTIONS

5. Are my prayers communication with God or a one-sided conversation?

6. Do I know how to listen to God's voice?

7. Do I know how God speaks to me?

REFLECTIONS

REFLECTIONS

> "...take every thought captive..."

CHAPTER 6
FORTIFY THE MIND

In Genesis chapter three, we see the story of the fall of man. At the start of this chapter, the enemy comes to man and plants a seed of doubt; verse one says; *"Now the serpent was more crafty (subtle, skilled in deceit) than any living creature of the field which the Lord God had made. And the serpent (Satan) said to the woman,* **"Can it really be that God has said,** *'You shall not eat from any tree of the garden'?"*

The moment Satan questioned what God had told them, and Eve (the woman) allowed that seed of doubt to enter and take root in her mind, the consequences were devastating!

Many times, thoughts will enter our mind but not every thought is ours. The enemy will always come to question what God has said - to plant seeds of doubt, seeds of temptation, seeds of discord. That's why the Bible says, *"casting down imaginations"* and *"bringing every thought into captivity to the obedience of Christ."* (2 Corinthians 10:5)

The word for "casting down" in the original Greek is "*kathaireo*" meaning to take down by force or violence, to demolish, to overthrow, to destroy.

To take captive means to hold as a prisoner, to confine, to control, to be kept within bounds.

"For though we walk in the flesh, we do not war according to the flesh. For the weapons of our warfare are not carnal but mighty in God for pulling down strongholds, casting down imaginations and every high thing that exalts itself against the knowledge of God, bringing every thought into captivity to the obedience of Christ," (2 Corinthians 10:3-5)

Renewing of the Mind

Romans 12:2 (AMP) says, *"And do not be conformed to this world [any longer with its superficial values and customs], but be transformed and progressively changed [as you mature spiritually] by the renewing of your mind [focusing on godly values and ethical attitudes], so that you may prove [for yourselves] what the will of God is, that which is good and acceptable and perfect [in His plan and purpose for you]."*

The dictionary meaning of "renewing" means to make like new, to restore, to renovate, to increase the life of or replace something old!

Phillipians 4:8 teaches us to, *"fix our minds on whatever is true, whatever is noble, whatever is just, whatever is pure, and lovely, and admirable. Think about things that are excellent and worthy of praise."*

When we renew our mind, we become aware of our thoughts, identify those which contradict God's truth, take the negative thoughts captive, replace them with the truth of His Word and then fix our minds back on the positive, the truth, the pure. It's an ongoing journey of learning and growing, allowing the Word to shape our thinking and our perspective. Renewing the mind leads to an inner transformation that will impact our desires and our actions.

We do not have to think about every thought that comes into our minds. We can choose what we dwell on. We can think things on purpose. Proverbs 23:7 says, *"As a man thinks in his heart, so is he."* What we think on will shape the actions we take.

As we spend time with the Lord and in His Word, our mind is being renewed, and we will be able to recognise what thoughts do not agree or line up with the truth. Then, when those thoughts come, immediately take them captive and replace them with truth.

One thing you can do each day is think about what God's word says about you - His love for you, His good plans for your future. Speak them out, write them down and read them every day.

Renewing your mind, then, is the process of getting back to your original position in Christ by interrupting the interruptions.

For example, to renew your mind from feeling fearful, think on and declare 2 Timothy 1:7: *"I have not been given a spirit of fear, but I have power, love and a sound mind."* Or to renew your mind when confronted with condemnation, think on and declare a verse like 2 Corinthians 5:21: *"I am the righteousness of God in Christ."*

Oftentimes, our mind has to be rewired after years of old patterns. That's what thinking and speaking truth does—it literally "rewires" or "renews" your brain, which takes time. So be patient but persistent and be sure to give yourself plenty of grace!

QUESTIONS

1. Do I understand how to renew my mind?

2. What are some lies that I have been believing and what truths can I replace these lies with?

3. What are some scriptures that I can meditate on in this season?

REFLECTIONS

REFLECTIONS

"...do not bypass the crushing..."

CHAPTER 7
OIL IN OUR LAMPS

In the parable of the wise and foolish virgins in Matthew 25, the oil represents the Holy Spirit and our personal relationship with Him.

I touched on this back in chapter one and mentioned the difference between the Person of the Holy Spirit and the *power* of the Holy Spirit.

In order to get the power and anointing (or oil) of the Holy Spirit, we must spend time with the Person of the Holy Spirit.

We cannot rely on corporate gatherings to experience His presence. To become intimate with Him we need to be with Him in the secret place, just us and Him!

When we look at the picture of the lamp, we can't see inside the earthen vessel. The rest of the wick, which we can see at the spout, is actually soaking in the oil contained inside.

As long as the lamp stays full of oil, the flame will be sustained by burning the oil - not burning the wick itself. The wick simply acts as a conduit to draw up the oil; the constant flow of oil keeps the wick cool, preventing it from burning itself.

However, there are a number of things that can cause the wick to burn out:

-If the wick is not properly saturated or the oil level is too low, the wick itself will dry out and be exposed to the flame causing it to burn very quickly.

- If you use incorrect oil for your lamp or wick, it will cause problems. Some oils may be too thick or too thin for the wick, affecting the wick's ability to draw it up.

- If the oil is contaminated (with water or other substances), it will not burn properly which can also damage the wick, causing it to burn itself. If the lamp has not been regularly cleaned it can also cause contamination of the oil.

- If the wick is too long, it can become dry or brittle at the top, making it susceptible to burning.

How does this relate to us?

The earthen vessel represents our human body which contains the treasure of Gods power and grace. 2 Corinthians 4:7 (AMP) says, *"But we have this precious treasure [the good news about salvation] in [unworthy] earthen vessels [of human frailty], so that the grandeur and surpassing greatness of the power will be [shown to be] from God [His sufficiency] and not from ourselves."*

The wick represents us (our inner man) as we yield to Holy Spirit, just as the wick draws the oil to the flame. If we don't keep ourselves saturated in the oil of His presence, we too will burn out. If we find ourselves becoming agitated or losing our peace, perhaps it's time to trim the wick? If we find we are doing things in our own strength, perhaps it's time to get more oil?

Galatians 3:3 says, *"Are you so foolish? Having begun in the Spirit, are you now being made perfect by the flesh?"* We cannot run this race in our own strength. In Zechariah 4:6 it says, *"... 'not by might, nor by power but by My Spirit' says the Lord".*

We cannot use other people's oil; we must get our own. In the parable of the wise and foolish virgins, Jesus emphasises this fact. Not all lamps and wicks are the same, just as we are not all the same. When the Word speaks of getting our own oil, we read that the foolish virgins asked the wise for some of their oil, but they answered, *"go and buy some oil for yourselves"* (Matthew 25:9). The oil is not something that can be shared, it is something we must obtain ourselves, sometimes through crushing.

Don't use fake or contaminated oil - are we watering down our oil? Are we using other substances, trying to fulfil what only God can? Are we regularly checking ourselves, cleaning out anything that shouldn't be there?

The process of extracting olive oil from olives requires crushing. The olives must pass through a press where they writhe and wrestle under pressure to produce the oil that feeds, illuminates, and heals.

This process of crushing olives to extract oil serves as a metaphor for the crushing through testing, trials and hardships individuals may face in life because it's in this process – journeying through life with the Holy Spirit, facing temptations, overcoming difficult obstacles, pushing through the challenges, making the right choices, choosing to be a living sacrifice for His glory, allowing Him to shape and mould us into all He has called us to be - that is where we develop our own oil.

On the evening of His betrayal, Jesus retreats to pray at the Mount of Olives in the Garden of Gethsemane, a place that literally means olive press or olive yard. He could have spent that night anywhere He wanted to, but instead, the Anointed One spends His last night on earth amoung olive trees, wrestling with the Father about His mission and destiny.

Jesus knows the raw brutality of what lies ahead and begs for another way, any other way. The acute anxiety crushes His body from the inside out as Jesus begins to sweat drops of blood.

"Father, if You are willing take this cup from me," Jesus petitions in Luke 22:42, but there is no response. Jesus then yields to the silence and surrenders to the Fathers intention: *"...yet not My will, but Yours be done."*

From here, Jesus walks the long road of obedience toward death. Before Jesus bled on the cross, He bled in the olive garden. Just as an olive must be crushed under intense pressure to yield oil, so too the Saviour of the world endured the intense pressure of crushing until the oil flowed...oil of grace, oil of mercy, oil of healing, oil of anointing.

Let this be a reminder to us all; do not bypass the crushing, don't skip the secret place, don't try and push through in our own strength, don't try and use someone else's oil. Let us trust in God's plan and choose His will over our own, knowing that He will produce something beautiful and powerful within us!

QUESTIONS

1. Is the oil in my lamp full?

2. Am I checking for contamination or watered down oil?

QUESTIONS

3. Are there any particular challenges/obstacles I am facing in this season?

4. What are some of the ways I keep myself full of the oil of the Spirit?

REFLECTIONS

REFLECTIONS

> "...we fight as victors.."

CHAPTER 8

FIGHTING FROM VICTORY

Romans 8: 37 says that we are more than conquerors through Christ.

It is so important to remember that we are fighting FROM victory not FOR victory! Jesus has already defeated the enemy. He has already conquered hell and death. However, whilst the victory is secured, it is not a passive stance. Believers are called to actively resist the devil, submit to God, and stand firm in faith, drawing on the power of Christ to overcome the enemy's attacks because they will still come.

There will be battles or challenges, but as believers we can face trials and temptations with the assurance that the ultimate victory has already been won. As we remain united with Christ and share in this victory, we are called to live from that place of authority and power. This means that we are not fighting to become victorious, but rather we are fighting as victors.

Deuteronomy 20:4 says, *"For the Lord your God is He who goes with you to fight for you against your enemies, to give you the victory."*

We fight until God's promises are manifested. We fight to enforce the victory that is already ours!

"Finally, my brethren, be strong in the Lord and in the power of HIS might." (Ephesians 6:10, emphasis added). This is not a fight that is done in our own strength, but in His alone.

God wants us to live a life of faith and victory. In Exodus 14:14, we are given a profound promise: *"The Lord himself will fight for you."* It is His will that we live victorious lives trusting in His truth, living under His authority.

Below are 7 keys to walking in victory:

1. We walk in victory when we remove the impurity of sin. (Job 11:14-15)

2. We walk in victory when we (not just read), but meditate, memorise and obey God's word.

(2 Timothy 3:16-17)

3. We walk in victory when we focus on God, fixing our gaze on Him alone and turning away from distractions. (Hebrews 12:2)

4. We walk in victory when we persevere through trials. (Galatians 6:9-10)

5. We walk in victory when we stand in faith. (Romans 5:3-5)

6. We walk in victory when we submit to God. (Job 22:2)

7. We walk in victory when we pray consistently. (Ephesians 6:18)

If we look at Hebrews 12:2 in the Amplified Bible it finishes by saying, ... *"and He sat down at the right hand of the throne of God [revealing His deity, His authority, and the completion of His work]."*

Jesus has defeated the enemy once and for all, His death and resurrection disarmed the power of Satan and his demons and while Satan's influence is still present in the world, his power has been broken. Colossians 2:15 says, *"Having disarmed principalities and powers, He made a public spectacle of them, triumphing over them in it."*

Satan has been stripped of his power and authority over us. We just need to walk in the authority of Christ by the power of the Holy Spirit and resist the enemy's lies.

QUESTIONS

1. What does it mean to be "more than a conqueror"?

2. Am I fighting in God's strength from victory or in my own strength?

3. From the 7 keys to walking in victory- what are 3 ways I can improve?

REFLECTIONS

REFLECTIONS

"we learn to discern the atmosphere"

CHAPTER 9

NATURALLY SUPERNATURAL

It is easy to walk into a room and know if someone is there. We are aware of their presence because of our senses; we can see them, we can hear them, we can smell them (their perfume or cologne, etc), we can touch them. We find ourselves far more aware of the natural or "seen" world of our humanity, than of the spiritual or "unseen" world and the Holy Spirit.

Training our spirit to be able to know the ways of God, to become more sensitive to the unseen realm, to the presence of the Holy Spirit, is so important to becoming the warrior God wants us to be.

When we walk into a room where a couple has just had an argument, we can generally feel the tension in the air. If we walk into a room full of people laughing, we can feel the joy! The same is true of the spiritual world, we just need to learn to discern the atmosphere. In some places this will be easy, others not so much, but practising this is extremely helpful when taking our place in God's army.

The spiritual or "unseen" realm is made evident throughout the word of God and as we deve-lop a sensitivity to this realm and understand that there are angels and demons at work beyond what we can see with our natural eyes, we will start to realise that we are on the winning side. There are thousands of angels protecting us, fighting for us and guiding us. Psalm 91:11-12 it says, *"For He shall give His angels charge over you, To keep you in all your ways. In their hands they shall bear you up, Lest you dash your foot against a stone."*

Once we realise that we have more on our side, we can rest assured that God's power and authority will protect His followers through both visible and invisible means.

"The servant of the man of God got up early and went out, and behold, there was an army with horses and chariots encircling the city. Elisha's servant said to him, "Oh no, my master! What are we to do?" Elisha answered, "Do not be afraid, for those who are with us are more than those who are with them." Then Elisha prayed and said, "Lord, please, open his eyes that he may see." And the Lord opened the servant's eyes and he saw; and behold, the mountain was full of horses and chariots of fire surrounding Elisha." (2 Kings 6:15-17 AMP)

Angels are powerful messengers of God, devoted to doing His will, and they serve as ministering spirits, protecting, delivering messages and fighting spiritual battles.

Even more than the angels though, being aware and sensitive to the Holy Spirit involves recognising and responding to Him, being attuned to His presence and promptings, whether through subtle nudging, strong convictions or a sense of peace or unease. We can learn to discern the Holy Spirit's guidance in various situations from major life decisions to everyday interactions.

Ask the Lord to open your eyes to the unseen, to increase your sensitivity to the Holy Spirit.

John 1:33 (AMP) says, *"I did not recognise Him [as the Messiah], but He who sent me to baptise in water said to me, 'He upon whom you see the Spirit descend and remain, this One is He who baptises with the Holy Spirit.'"*

Spend time with Him, get to know Him, pray, pursue holiness, practice His presence, actively seek to understand and obey His guidance.

Cultivate an ear to hear His voice - through the word of God, through prayer and through promptings within your spirit. Learn to recognise the different ways He communicates. Be patient and consistently practice these principles.

QUESTIONS

1. Am I aware of the unseen realm?

2. How can I become more sensitive to the Holy Spirit?

3. How can I grow in discernment?

REFLECTIONS

REFLECTIONS

CHAPTER 10

HABITS AND CHARACTERISTICS OF A WARRIOR OF GOD (RECAP + EXTRAS)

* Ensure your foundations are solid
* Prayer life - pray continually
* Be prepared - physically, mentally, spiritually
* Intimacy with the Lord - abide in the secret place
* Be Bold; stand for righteousness
* Know your target/enemy
* Teamwork - Unity with the Body of Christ (where there is unity, He commands a blessing), an army works together - strengthen and encourage one another
* Read the Word, meditate on the Word, obey the Word, put the Word into practice, speak the Word, be strengthened in the Word
* Fix your gaze on Christ alone
* Allow growth through pruning and correction
* Be a man or woman of integrity...other people may not see everything, but God does
* Use the armour God has given you
* Stand firm; back in Ephesians where we were reading about the armour, it says "having done all - to stand".
* Protect your mind
* Stay full of the oil of God - do not use substitutes
* Worship and praise - singing out truth - sometimes we sing because we're sure, other times we sing until we know but nevertheless, we sing the truth! Like the song says, *"this is how I fight my battles"*.
* Display the fruit of the Spirit - love, joy, peace, patience, kindness, goodness, faithfulness, gentleness, self control
* Get heavenly direction - what battles need to be fought and what has come just to distract or take you off course?
* Kingdom view - we are seated in heavenly places, look from the perspective of Heaven
* Aim to finish well - "I have fought the good fight, I have finished the race, I have kept the faith." (2 Timothy 4:7)

QUESTIONS

1. What are some other habits or characteristics of a warrior of God?

2. In what ways have I grown as a warrior throughout this study?

REFLECTIONS

REFLECTIONS

REFLECTIONS

ADDITIONAL NOTES

ADDITIONAL NOTES

ADDITINAL NOTES

ADDITIONAL NOTES

ADDITIONAL NOTES

ADDITIONAL NOTES

ADDITIONAL NOTES

ADDITIONAL NOTES

ADDITIONAL NOTES

ADDITIONAL NOTES

ADDITIONAL NOTES

ADDITIONAL NOTES

www.ingramcontent.com/pod-product-compliance
Lightning Source LLC
Chambersburg PA
CBHW061821290426
44110CB00027B/2935